DISCOVER YOUR INFINITE POSSIBILITIES

Spirit Children of God Having a Mortal Experience

God's Game of Love

by Lou Principe

DISCOVER YOUR INFINITE POSSIBILITIES

Second Edition 2019

No part of this book may be reproduced in any written or electronic form, recording, or photocopying without written permission of the author or publisher. The exception would be in the case of brief quotations embedded in the critical articles or reviews and pages where permission is specifically granted by the author or publisher.

Although every precaution has been taken to verify the accuracy of the information contained herein, the author or publisher assume no responsibility for any errors or omissions. No liability is assumed for damages that may result from the use of information contained within.

Library of Congress Catalog Number: 2014920466

Spirit Children Having a Mortal Experience
Louis Principe
ISBN 978-0-9850269-7-4

1. Spirituality
2. Self-help
3. New Age
4. Metaphysical, Natural Healing
5. Spiritual Exercises for Spiritual Growth

DISCOVER YOUR INFINITE POSSIBILITIES
Acknowledgments

I wish to thank my father, Frank Principe, who worked three shifts a day at the Waldorf Astoria and the Savoy Hilton to feed his family. Through his work ethic, he became my role model of hard work, discipline, and service to the family.

My maternal grandfather, Rocco Savino, made many sacrifices when migrating from Italy to the United States during World War I to save his four daughters from falling prey to Mussolini's soldiers. He delivered ice for $2.00 a week because he couldn't speak English. I owe my very life to his dedication to family.

My paternal grandfather, Casper Principe, after whom I am named, was adopted by the Krauss family in Kingston, New York as a baby during World War I. They brought him from Italy to France and then to the United States. He is named after St. Casper of Italy, who worked with prisoners and the afflicted during times of the plague and later died of the plague. I thank him for my name and possible bloodline.

I wish to thank Jack Gazzardo, who presented the very first sales training seminar I attended based on the Xerox Training system which most
companies adopted.

I thank all the authors of the books I have read, instructors of seminars I've attended, and the many professors throughout the world whose teachings I have compiled to write this book. There are too many to list individually.

I give thanks to all the leaders of the houses of worship whom I interviewed.

Finally, I wish to thank all the people I have encountered throughout my life, particularly those who challenged my ideas, it strengthened my resolve.

DISCOVER YOUR INFINITE POSSIBILITIES

DEDICATION

Albert Einstein in one of his last talks at UCLA told a group of professors that there is a Higher Being who created many universes. This book is dedicated to that Higher Being.

DISCOVER YOUR INFINITE POSSIBILITIES
INTRODUCTION

I teach Epistemology - the Science of Knowledge - in other words, What people think they know and how they know it. I also teach how to unlearn false information by replacing it with universal truths. My job is to jar people out of their mental comfort zones enough to open their minds to exploring all the possibilities they have. Most people have been programmed to live within a certain set of comfort parameters and to conform to those parameters. We box ourselves in like photographs in picture frames. My assignment on this earth is to facilitate the expansion of human awareness.

I have been teaching transformational learning for over fifty years. This type of learning involves unlearning and forsaking deeply held assumptions and beliefs embedded in the mind since childhood and consciously replacing them with timeless truths that have been hidden from us. I help people develop these new ways of thinking so they can achieve their true potential. If you read with an open mind and heart, you will find this book to be educational, inspirational, and motivational. You will find things inside yourself that you didn't know existed.

We are an amalgam of the traditions embedded within us as children. We learn from parents, friends, teachers, religious leaders, and life experiences.

Most of us have been singularly cultured and are living in a world of perception we mistake for reality. People don't know what they don't know. A foreign language is foreign until we have learned the language. Some of us have subconsciously built scotomas or blind spots. We don't see or know some things because we never paid attention to them. We left those pieces of information for others to act upon trusting their judgments, in today's society it's a big mistake. What people don't know may kill them, their family, and future generations.

The juncture between the emotional and cognitive aspects of learning poses the biggest challenge for those seeking to learn both effectively and continuously. Both inspiration and motivation – even more so

DISCOVER YOUR INFINITE POSSIBILITIES

than any cognitive aspects of the learner's situation - must be present for learning to be impacted. Reading this book will create ideas in your mind that will encourage you to think outside the box, accept challenges, and stretch your sometimes recalcitrant, stubborn mind.

Think of your comfort zone as a room thermostat. If the thermostat is set at 78 degrees, you are comfortable. This book will ask you to lower or raise the temperature on your mental thermostat to cause you enough mental discomfort to examine critically your choices and thought patterns.

As humans living on this earth, we have been locked into traditions taught to us as children. Failing to examine the limiting nature of these traditions prevents us from seeing all the options available to us. I am asking you, the reader, to step outside of your comfort zone to expand your options.

DISCOVER YOUR INFINITE POSSIBILITIES
YOUR PRIOR PROGRAMMING

Your prior programming and attitude are all that prevent you from living life to its fullest. We all must become humble to become teachable. Of the thousands of people who have attended my classes and seminars, I have received hundreds of letters all documenting the uniqueness of this mind-opening program and the outstanding results the attendees achieved.

This book encapsulates the principles from which this program was created. It will not only help you spiritually, but once applied, it will lead you to a higher intelligence level which will also help you a ccomplish anything in life, provided it is a Godly goal.

Centuries ago Aristotle taught us that we are nothing but a habit. We are so programmed that we carry out actions automatically without thinking about what we are doing. We confuse activity with accomplishment.

We have been doing things habitually for years because we have been brainwashed by those in control, they permitted the FDA to put chemicals in our water and food supply. According to Harvard University, the most toxic runoff of an aluminum factory is fluoride, it acts like a magnet and goes to the Pineal Gland, the most important gland in your body according to Doctor Oz, "it controls all the other glands, it calcifies it.Turns it into a rock.

Why do you think cancer is growing so rapidly when hundreds of billions of dollars are supporting research? Haven't they figured it out? Don't inject poisonous chemicals in our food and water supply, it dumbs down our intellectual level, Google Washington Post, The Dumbing of America), and spiritual connection to the God who created us. Fluoride causes Spiritual Amnesia

The Biggest secret religions don't want you to know about:

Clean Up Your Pineal Gland and have a direct connection to The Almighty.

DISCOVER YOUR INFINITE POSSIBILITIES
YOU DON'T NEED ANYONE BETWEEN YOUR CREATOR AND YOU.

As human being, we are nothing but energy. Energy will always exist in different forms. Right now, you are in human form. You have tiny crystals in your pineal gland which vibrate with A Higher Power. Anyone can achieve it within a 30 day period. Read what Harvard has to say.

Harvard Research Finds Link Between Fluoridated Water, ADHD & Mental Disorders

Published on March 5, 2014
By Joe Martino
47.9K shares

The fact is, fluoride is a known developmental neurotoxin and practices of water fluoridation have long been proven to be ineffective. If individuals choose to use fluoridated tooth paste or choose fluoride treatments at their dental office, that is acceptable but two things should happen:

1. People should be taught about the harmful effects of fluoride and the damage it can cause to your teeth and your body.

2. Water fluoridation should be stopped everywhere immediately as it is nothing more than a legal way for chemical companies to get rid of toxic waste while profiting.

Fluoride accumulates in the body over time, so even though the amounts being ingested might be small each time, it builds up over years and can cause serious health issues. Research has found that fluoride affects normal endocrine function, causes kidney disease, bone weakness, dental fluorosis, cancer, lowering of IQ, calcification of the pineal gland, arthritis, immune deficiencies, skeletal fluorosis and much more.

Sources:
1. http://www.thelancet.com/journals/laneur/article/PIIS1474-4422(13)70278-3/abstract

How did the Germans control the Jews in 1938 before World War Two?

They put fluoride in the ghetto drinking water.. It makes people Complacent, it dumbs people down and turns them into working slaves. When we liberated the Jews from the concentration camps, we fond vats and vats of fluoride.
The same year China signed a contract to fluoridate the waters in the United States.
Edwin Barney, Sigmund Frauds nephew went to the President and told him he will guarantee him the election. He knows how to control people's minds.

There was an organization formed called B.R.I.C., Brazil, Russia, India and China to take over the United States by using a very slow Machiavellian Plan.

DISCOVER YOUR INFINITE POSSIBILITIES

A Machiavellian Plan was a secret document ordered by the Pope in the 15th Century on how to take control of the world by programming people's minds.

They found with experience, it takes about 70 years before new programming sets in. Teach them when they are young so when they grew up, they will think everything is real life and if someone approaches them later in life with a new idea or invention, their first thought is No, I'm not interested. Programmed as a child. You hear the word NO thousands of times as children. Besides, you don't want to think about it, even though it may make you r life better. Programmed like I was growing up, not to talk about politics, religion or how much you make. Why is everything a big secret? Why keep people in the dark. We are all going to die and report what we have done with our lives?

The Prince by Machiavelli is a short story on how to take political control of a country. Instead of warring with our enmity lets be friends and slowly take them over, they are so greedy, they'll buy everything.

The only difference between us and mental asylum patients is that we get to go home at night while they don't!

And right now, it's God's time to warn the Earth, it's got only 40 more years before the east coast is flooded. Look at the facts. The Final Judgment may come then or soon after.

A wise person learns from others. A fool has to experience things for themselves. I have been a fool most of my life. I finally realize now that I am the potter and the clay is me! We mold ourselves from ideas, life experiences, and what we think we know or don't know. If you get nothing else out of this book, please remember to explore all possibilities with an open mind and then decide for yourself what is true. You will need to sift through what your parents, friends, employers, cultures, educators, and the government tells you.
You cannot truly trust anyone in life, not even in the house of worship you attend, as religious leaders have grown up in traditions, as well.

DISCOVER YOUR INFINITE POSSIBILITIES

Of the multitude of feedback I have received from those who have attended our programs, one comment has always stood out.

118 Oaks Circle
Port Richey, Florida
33568

KAY STEVENS
SALES CONSULTANT

U.S. HOME CORPORATION

Phone: (813) 868-9475
Toll Free From Pinellas: (813) 442-3583

US·HOME

8/3/85

Dear Lou,

I hated you 3 weeks ago — now I'm thanking you for making me uncomfortable enough to examine my weak areas. You "unstuck" me and I'm on the way toward becoming the achiever that I am.

Sincerely,
Kay

"I hated you when I first met you, but you unstuck me. Thank you."

DISCOVER YOUR INFINITE POSSIBILITIES

People waste their time on unimportant things instead of focusing on what matters most. Most of us are afraid of our potential. My mission is to help you unlock that potential and become a free thinker so you can discover **your infinite possibilities.**

Lou

DISCOVER YOUR INFINITE POSSIBILITIES
WHY I WROTE THIS BOOK: My Personal History

God has permitted me to witness and participate in many miracles. My life is a progression of miracles. Before I was born, my father had a ruptured appendix. During the emergency surgery, the doctor concluded they could not save him, so they closed the incision with 42 steel staples instead of stitching him normally, not expecting him to live through the night. A Catholic priest was called to give my father the Last Rites. But my father did not die. Miraculously, he survived the night and lived another fifty years. I owe my very existence to this first miracle.

My mother – already with two small children in tow and feeling the weight of the extra burden of a third during World War II – tried to abort me in the womb. Fortunately, the attempt was unsuccessful. I have the scar on top of my head from the coat hanger to remind me of how fortunate I am to be alive.

This was the second miracle.

When I was 17 I was involved in a car accident that put me in the hospital in traction for weeks. Before surgery, I had my first out of body experience. I remember floating to the ceiling and out of the room, down the hallway, and above the nurses' station. I was more than frightened! I was panicked and tried with all my might to ye "Help! Help!" but no one could hear me.

DISCOVER YOUR INFINITE POSSIBILITIES

After I returned to my body, I didn't speak of that experience for years because I thought people would think I was crazy. I had never heard the term "out of body experience." But this turned out to be the third miracle of my very existence.

Years later, my oldest daughter Louise was born with the umbilical cord wrapped around her neck. She was not breathing and had turned blue. The doctors tried to revive her for several minutes and were about to give up when another doctor entered the room, grabbed her by the ankles, and rapidly and repeatedly slapped her back until a plug came out of her mouth and she started crying. I count this as yet one more miracle in my amazing life journey.

My youngest daughter Victoria had no vital signs after the car collided with a garbage truck.

The emergency crew told me that she had no vital signs. However, they didn't give up on her and brought her back to life after working for ninety minutes. I bless the E.M.T.s in Clermont, Florida for not giving up on her. Because of their heroic efforts, she is alive today. This is another in a series of incredible events in my life and the lives of family members.

At seven years of age, my son Joey was diagnosed with a malignant brain tumor. We were told he wouldn't live through the surgery to remove it. During the operation, the doctor called and said,
"I can't explain what happened, but your son is going to live a

DISCOVER YOUR INFINITE POSSIBILITIES
normal and healthy life.

He said he would explain it to me after he left the operating room. He later told me, "After I called and told you to prepare for the worst, it is as if God put His hand in your son's brain and lifted the tumor out with all the roots."

In 2001 I had a heart attack and a stroke with resulting complications. My income dwindled from $2,000 a day from my consulting business down to $1,200 a month from disability payments. By the grace of God, because I always paid my taxes and tithing, the Lord provided and I always had enough. This crisis taught me to become desireless, and now I know the difference between wants and needs.

On New Years' Eve 2011, I was taken once again to the emergency room with chest pain where the cardiac surgeon immediately scheduled me for a bypass and valve replacement surgery. I received a message which I believe to be by divine intervention directing me to see a different doctor at another facility in New Orleans.
The original cardiac surgeon told me I was crazy when I told him I had received a message from God to see another doctor.

Nevertheless, I went to see Dr. Parrino, who prior to surgery, had a cardiac catheterization, angiogram performed through my left wrist. They lost me on the table. I remember them screaming; "Lou wake up, wake up", when I opened my eyes, they told me I had stopped breathing and thought they lost me.

The Dr. Parrino informed me that if I had received the bypass, I would be dead by now. It turned out miraculously my body made its collateral bypass. I was operated on in April 2011 at the Ochsner Hospital, but the surgeon replaced only my calcified aortic valve, the real root of the problem. This was yet another escape from death.

In October 2011, just six months after the open-heart surgery, I was involved in a very severe automobile accident. I heard metal crashing, I saw the airbag coming at me in slow motion,

DISCOVER YOUR INFINITE POSSIBILITIES

though airbags typically deploy at over 200 miles per hour. The next thing I knew I was outside the car looking at my skeleton behind the wheel. I knew I was dead, but this time I wasn't frightened like I had been the last time. I felt very peaceful, and at that precise moment, I received transcendental knowledge directly from God. This book is my attempt at channeling that direct knowledge, as I feel my life and the lives of my family have been spared because God intended for me to share this divine message with you.

I know without reservation that this is my mission. It has taken 74 years for God to mold me with life experiences to write this book for you.

After my son's doctor used the word "miracle" to describe his escape from death, I promised God I would dedicate the rest of my life to doing His work. I developed real estate and customer service seminars that were based on spiritual, Biblical teachings. I have now spent over fifty years developing and teaching dynamic, life-changing seminars that have helped not only corporations and government agencies, but also the poor, the prison population, the unemployed, and the underemployed. The results of these programs are well documented.
Participants and organizations experience an immediate increase in productivity, teamwork, and employee retention. For the prison population the recidivism rate dropped dramatically. These results are the evidence that God is using me to fulfill His mission, just as you too will find your divinely inspired mission.

DISCOVER YOUR INFINITE POSSIBILITIES
WE DON'T LIVE IN A PERFECT WORLD.

But we can help make it better. Our society based on free enterprise keeps the collars around our necks and jerks the chain every thirty days. The system revolves around money. The car, mortgage, insurance, utility bills, and credit card bills must be paid every month. Is this logical?

Those who exercise unrighteous dominion, acquire power over others, which is why 75% of the workforce hate their jobs. This is something we all take for granted in modern society. Perhaps one of the reasons you are drawn to this book is that you would like to get off the treadmill.

But you don't know-how?

The qualities of leadership are the same in all fields, the leader being the one who sets the highest example! As an organization tries to expand, what takes place is a fatal shift from leadership to management which marks the plateaus and failures of most organizations. Most CEOs are great leaders. They have mastered the art of self-management.

Some managers, however, like safe ships in port. The nature of management is that they don't make waves however, battleships were made to fight. No one ever managed anyone into battle.
A leader has a passion for equality. We think of great leaders like David and Alexander,

DISCOVER YOUR INFINITE POSSIBILITIES

though airbags typically deploy at over 200 miles per hour. The next thing I knew I was outside the car looking at my skeleton behind the wheel. I knew I was dead, but this time I wasn't frightened like I had been the last time. I felt very peaceful, and at that precise moment, I received transcendental knowledge directly from God. This book is my attempt at channeling that direct knowledge, as I feel my life and the lives of my family have been spared because God intended for me to share this divine message with you.

I know without reservation that this is my mission. It has taken 74 years for God to mold me with life experiences to write this book for you.

After my son's doctor used the word "miracle" to describe his escape from death, I promised God I would dedicate the rest of my life to doing His work. I developed real estate and customer service seminars that were based on spiritual, Biblical teachings. I have now spent over fifty years developing and teaching dynamic, life-changing seminars that have helped not only corporations and government agencies, but also the poor, the prison population, the unemployed, and the underemployed. The results of these programs are well documented.

Participants and organizations experience an immediate increase in productivity, teamwork, and employee retention. For the prison population the recidivism rate dropped dramatically. These results are the evidence that God is using me to fulfill His mission, just as you too will find your divinely inspired mission.

DISCOVER YOUR INFINITE POSSIBILITIES
WE DON'T LIVE IN A PERFECT WORLD.

But we can help make it better. Our society based on free enterprise keeps the collars around our necks and jerks the chain every thirty days. The system revolves around money. The car, mortgage, insurance, utility bills, and credit card bills must be paid every month. Is this logical?

Those who exercise unrighteous dominion, acquire power over others, which is why 75% of the workforce hate their jobs. This is something we all take for granted in modern society. Perhaps one of the reasons you are drawn to this book is that you would like to get off the treadmill.

But you don't know-how?

The qualities of leadership are the same in all fields, the leader being the one who sets the highest example! As an organization tries to expand, what takes place is a fatal shift from leadership to management which marks the plateaus and failures of most organizations. Most CEOs are great leaders. They have mastered the art of self-management.

Some managers, however, like safe ships in port. The nature of management is that they don't make waves however, battleships were made to fight. No one ever managed anyone into battle.
A leader has a passion for equality. We think of great leaders like David and Alexander,

DISCOVER YOUR INFINITE POSSIBILITIES

who shared their beans and water with their men, called them by name, marched along with them in the heat, slept out on the ground with them, and they were first over the wall. To the manager, on the other hand, the very idea of equality is repugnant and even counterproductive. Perks, promotion, and power are the name of the game. Awe and reverence for rank is everything. We need to have more emphasis on teaching leadership. Currently, men who delight their superiors get the high command, while the men who delight the lower ranks receive reprimands.

Leaders are movers and shakers, inventive, creative, original, unpredictable, and full of surprises that discomfort the enemy (the manager), in war and the main office in peace.

The average manager is a safe, conservative, predictable, conforming, organizational man. Where would management be without the inflexible paper processing, dress standards, attention to the proper social, political, and vigilant watch over habits and attitudes that gratify the stockholders and satisfy security?

"If you love me," said the greatest of all leaders, "keep my Commandments', "If you know what is good for you, "says the manager, "you will keep my Commandments and not make waves." That is why the rise of management in corporations normally marks a decline in profits, in governments, increase in taxes.

Management does not hire or promote individuals who threaten their positions, and so as the power of management spreads even wider, the quality deteriorates, if that is possible.

True leaders are inspiring because they are inspired, caught up in a higher purpose, devoid of personal ambition, idealistic, and incorruptible. There is necessarily some of the manager in every leader. Conversely, there should be some of the leaders in every manager. So vast is the discrepancy between management and leadership, that only a blind man guess them backward, yet that is what we do. (taken from a magazine article).

DISCOVER YOUR INFINITE POSSIBILITIES

For fifty years we will be customers of a phone or electric company. If we don't pay our bills within thirty days, we will have our services turned off even though we need the utility. These companies know we have no choice but to use them. Regardless of the equity we have in our homes which we worked hard to acquire if we get sick and miss three months of mortgage payments, the banks foreclose, and the attorneys' fees accumulate into the thousands. Most of us cannot afford to give up our jobs to change careers or start businesses because we find ourselves on this endless treadmill of living paycheck to paycheck. Do you think this is how humans are intended to live?

We are given earthly life to experience joy and happiness. However, most people today are in bondage, perhaps not literally like the Jews in ancient Egypt, but mentally. As the Jews accepted their lot of slavery, so do most people accept their mental enslavement; only we do not call it slavery today – we call it "free enterprise." What is free about having to work every day to make mortgage and tax payments every month?

There is a way off the treadmill. It involves a shift in our focus from the material to the spiritual. The remainder of the book is devoted to how this can be accomplished and why this refocusing is so powerful.

We can break free of these invisible bonds and accomplish anything in life provided we are willing to allow God to take the reins! Like playing the lottery, we can wait and see if we are in the one in ten million who hits the jackpot, or we can invite God to take charge of our lives and watch our blessings accumulate.

DISCOVER YOUR INFINITE POSSIBILITIES
YOU DON'T NEED AN INTERMEDIARY BETWEEN YOU AND YOUR HIGHER POWER.

There have been many avatars – spirits of God in human form – throughout history who came here to teach for the good of humankind. But we are so indoctrinated into the religious traditions that we have been programmed to invalidate all others. We are taught to believe other religions are cults and ours is the one true religion.

We were taught to believe that our God is the only God and that our religion is the only true religion. This is a falsity perpetrated by early churches to control the minds of the masses and the political stage while increasing their wealth.

All the spiritual teachers – Christ, Mohammed, Buddha, etc. – came along to guide us toward a correct spiritual life. Their messages are all the same and can be boiled down to one central tenet: loving and not harming one another.

For this book, I refer often to Christ and his teachings because that is my path; thus, I believe it is also valid to use Christ as an intermediary in your prayers. I use Christ's teachings often to illustrate various points, as I find the teachings to be powerful and useful. I wish to be clear that I do not believe Christianity to be the only true religion because I am less familiar with others.

These writings are spiritual and often refer to God or Jesus Christ. I often make Biblical references and mention Christ's teachings, as this is the path to which I subscribe. However, please substitute whatever you consider to be your Higher Power, even if it is "the universe," as I believe that all spiritual paths lead to the goal of oneness with Source or God or whatever you consider as your Higher Power, as long as the motivation is not to control or exploit earthly resources or beings. You may also find I use words such as "He" and "Him" to describe God or Christ. These words – born from a patriarchal culture admittedly – are used only for simplicity.
My sincere hope is that the reader will read past the pronouns and specific names for God, Source, Creator, or Higher Power to

DISCOVER YOUR INFINITE POSSIBILITIES
glean the spiritual and practical messages imbued in these words.

Please note that I also refer to the afterlife, as this concept is key to understanding the wisdom offered here. If you do not believe in heaven, reincarnation, or any sort of afterlife, I ask only that you suspend your beliefs and judgments while reading that you may consider the concepts presented to you in the following pages.

DISCOVER YOUR INFINITE POSSIBILITIES
HISTORY OF WORLD RELIGIONS

Before I discuss our connection with God, I would like to give a simplistic history of world religions. New churches were founded by first destroying the original teachings of Christ and other prophets, rewriting their Scriptures, and disallowing all people to read the original Scriptures. They began killing hundreds of thousands of people in the name of God, and the soldiers returned to Rome with heads on their spears to spark fear in the masses. In the name of God, the Church took money from the people they killed and forced Jews, Muslims, and Pagans to join the Church or be killed. What happened centuries ago is still happening today!

The modern Church exerts control over its members through instilling fear. Today we have Mega churches whose real estate is worth millions and whose leaders fly by private jets and live in mansions while people are starving outside. Modern religion equates to membership and membership equates to money.

Christ taught us that we are easily led astray. It is wise to refrain from having blind faith in anyone or anything except God or the prophet to whom you subscribe, in the case of Christianity, Jesus Christ. You cannot rely on your pastor to save you when that pastor may need saving himself!

DISCOVER YOUR INFINITE POSSIBILITIES
ORIGINAL TEACHINGS OF CHRIST

The Nag Hammadi documents are a collection of Coptic papyrus manuscripts dating back to Christ's time, not 300 years after His death. They were discovered in 1945 in the Egyptian desert near the the town of Nag Hammadi. For years these documents were kept in a locked vault where armed guards watched over them.

There are thirteen manuscripts including conversations from Christ to the apostles. In total, each comprising a library of forty-two tractates, not all of which are fully preserved. Presumably, all of these writings are translated from the original Greek. Most – but not all – of the documents are Gnostic or esoteric, and therefore, shed considerable light on the history and character of the Gnostic religion of antiquity.

A brief definition of Gnosticism from Merriam Webster is :
"the thought and practice especially of various cults of
late pre-Christian and early Christian centuries distinguished by the conviction that matter is evil and that emancipation comes through esoteric knowledge of spiritual truth held to be essential to salvation."

Before the discovery of these ancient documents, most of our knowledge of Gnosticism was dependent upon the writings of opponents, especially the church founders. You can find the Nag Hammadi books in most libraries, and you are invited to research them for yourself.

The Church started venerating saints in the 15th century which led to the worship of false idols. There is a conversation in the Nag Hammadi documents between Jesus Christ and Peter where Jesus says, "Someday, people will be praying to you" to which Peter responds, "Oh no My Lord."

In an interview with Bill Maher, a church official admitted that people are stupid enough to pray to statues. They are idols!
We are meant to pray directly to God and not people.

DISCOVER YOUR INFINITE POSSIBILITIES

In today's society, the government is supposed to operate independently of any religion. But in Christ's time, they were intertwined, so priests were also politicians. This merging of church and state had been operating a few thousand years before Christ's appearance on the scene. Therefore, it never occurred to anyone that it should be any different.

Many European cultures were originally based on the union of church and state. Constantine set the mold for Western culture when he declared himself head of the Roman Catholic Church, thereby recognizing no separation between church and state. Throughout the Middle Ages it was assumed that any monarch was also a high priest who pledged his allegiance to the Papacy. Atrocities and abuses were rampant within this system as leaders began using the church for political gain as they try to do today..

The integration of religion and government was successfully broken by the American Revolution when it would be decided there would be no state religion, thereby assuring religious freedom. However, widespread religious groups still try to exert power over the political domain.

In Alabama, some pastors are paid thousands a month by Alabama's ADECA as government agents to control their flock. The parishioners are told who they should vote for BY THEIR PASTOR.

DISCOVER YOUR INFINITE POSSIBILITIES
OUR MISSION ON EARTH

We are God's spiritual children, and we were permitted to com into this world to test our love for Him.

Are we doing what we ought to be doing? *To fulfill the measure of our existence on this earth we must accomplish two tasks: First, we must discover our mission in this earthly life. Second, we must fulfill it with a sense of urgency.*

We must not get sidetracked by earthly illusions as evil forces (Satan) would have us do. This earth is an illusion. It is a play, and each of us is the main character. There is a war taking place. Satan would hold you back from reaching your true potential and thwart God's plan for you, your family, and future generations. Therefore, you must be the pioneer in your family and break the cycle of illusion. Once you internalize the principles set forth here, you will find the answers to most of your questions about God and your life on this planet.

We must continuously turn our thoughts to divine sovereignty and our human responsibility. Because of our righteous actions today, we will be blessed forever. We will receive the fullness of our blessings both in this earthly life and the afterlife if we remain committed to living righteous lives while we are here. The decisions we make today will have consequences throughout all eternity. Another way of saying this is that whatever we do today has a ripple effect into the future in the way throwing a pebble into a lake creates ripples across the water.

To delay reaching for heavenly concerns is inexcusable. The only road leading there is the shortest and most proper road. The purpose of this life is to perfect ourselves and overcome worldly matters. Even the smallest flaw will become a barrier to reaching our utmost potential. Any flaw, no matter how small, will hold us back in God's kingdom.

DISCOVER YOUR INFINITE POSSIBILITIES

The Marlboro House

A high rise condominium built in Winter Haven, Florida in the 1980's at the cost of several millions of dollars was condemned upon completion because there was a tiny flaw in the foundation. In time, the flaw became magnified, the weight of the building created a crevice in the foundation, and the entire building had to be demolished.

<u>Now is the time to rid ourselves of our flaws</u>.

DISCOVER YOUR INFINITE POSSIBILITIES
THERE ARE TWO WORLDS:
ONE LEADS US TO DESTRUCTION AND THE OTHER TO SALVATION.

Which do you choose? Most people possess the necessary skills to accomplish anything they want to in life, but since they don't realize who they are or their purpose in life, they never fulfill their destined path.

Has your mind been focused more on worldly things than spiritual things? Is your eye singular to worldly concerns, or is it singularly focused on God's glory? *One of the greatest sins of this world is the search for private gain at the expense of others.*

Have we lost our belief or our faith in our capacity to share the love of God to improve our lives and the lives of others? Each of us alone has the power to work in God's kingdom today. We can share with someone the love we have if we can focus our energy on God. If we face today's problems with righteous self-honesty, we will make the right choices.

Set a daily Godly goal and accomplish it. The small daily problems are what cause us to trip and fall. We are so busy trying to become someone else or living up to someone else's expectations that we fail to discover our true passion. If we take the time to explore God's mission for us, we will find that whatever we do to help others return to Him will inspire our passion.

We are taught to conform to the world. We are so concerned with paying tomorrow's debt that we miss today's sunset. Some of us are incapable of visualizing a future where we love one another and all the positives that will bring. If only we could treat each other as though we were all four years old, trying to help one another get back home, with no hidden agendas what a wonderful world this would be.

There is a serious battle being waged in our lives, and that battle is fought within our souls.

DISCOVER YOUR INFINITE POSSIBILITIES

Which side do you choose? We are born in the likeness of God the spirit. As spirits having human experiences, we are subject to temptations of the evil forces. As humans, we can justify stealing, murder, war, and even exploitation in the name of religion to enrich ourselves. We may have started with good intentions, but "my people are easily led astray."

With Spirit as our guide, we can experience the simple joys of being alive. We can decide that each day is ours to spend and that we will become the best people we can be. We can study about God and share the knowledge we gain with someone. The present is the eternal now. In the present moment, we plant the seed for all eternity.

DISCOVER YOUR INFINITE POSSIBILITIES
THE IMPORTANCE OF PHYSICAL HEALTH

Physical health and spiritual maturity go hand in hand.

When we feel well, we think more clearly. When we think clearly, we inevitably feel better physically, which in turn permits us to listen to the still small voice in our hearts, the spirit of God. The vessel we are given in this earthly life must be made pure if we are to function properly. If our body fails to function properly, our immune health and brain function will be compromised, as will the degree of influence Spirit may have upon us.

Here is a personal story to illustrate this point. Eighteen years ago I had restrictive lung disease; a heart attack; five coronary stents; back, neck, hip, knee, finger, and bilateral corporal tunnel surgeries. I weighed 317 pounds and was on a CPAP and an oxygen machine. After 9-11, I began volunteering my time giving free seminars to the unemployed, under-employed, and the prison population.

Through sharing my talents with others, the Spirit of Revelation was given to me. In three years, I regained my health, started eating correctly, and lost over a hundred pounds and kept it off. I learned the difference between God's food and man's food, God's medicine and man's medicine.

Proper Diet for Physical and Spiritual Health

There are numerous scriptural references in world religions to fasting for increasing spiritual strength. But prolonged fasting can be dangerous today due to the immediate release of chemicals in our bodies from the foods we eat and medicines we ingest. A fast can release these chemicals into our bloodstream, which can make us feel sick. Therefore, we need to tend to what we put into our bodies at all times and fast in moderation.

We cannot expect our cars to run smoothly if we don't take care of them. Putting in the proper grade of gas and oil alone will double the life of a car's engine. Similarly, what we put into our bodies affects how we function, how we think, and how long we live.

DISCOVER YOUR INFINITE POSSIBILITIES
The purity of our physical bodies dictates the clarity of our communication channel with Spirit.

Many people take drugs for diseases that can be cured or controlled through diet. Most drug have what is called a "half-life" or amount of time they stay in the system after ingestion. The instant effect of the drug occurs within one hour, but the average drug can remain in our system for up to six months! Not one doctor ever told me about the dangers of using drugs nor how habit-forming they are. I'm guessing this is the same for you. I spent over eight years in a fog while I was taking a variety of medications for my various illnesses. All I wanted to do was sleep. I couldn't concentrate; I kept forgetting things. I'd walk from one room to another asking myself why I went there. How many people you know are in this same situation, particularly older people who tend to take more medications? Most drugs dull our aliveness and clog our spiritual communication channel!

Our circulatory system gets clogged in the way old rusty pipes can get clogged. The blood cannot then flow freely to the entire body. According to Scriptures, theoretically, if we are bitten by a venomous snake, and if we have the proper spirit and body, the venom will not harm us. Rather, the venom will make its way to the liver where it is neutralized. The problem arises when blood channels are clogged with chemicals and impurities. The venom tries to reach the liver by rerouting itself through different canals. Unfortunately, it usually travels through the largest artery, the aorta, which leads directly to the heart. In this case, the person dies of a heart attack. If our circulatory channels are free of debris, the venom can flow directly to the liver where it would be neutralized.

The average person has four to six pounds of old fecal matter clogging the upper bowel preventing it from functioning properly; it may even be partially petrified. The circulatory system can be clogged by plaque, which is affected to a great extent by what we eat.

Toxins in food affect every major system in our bodies.

DISCOVER YOUR INFINITE POSSIBILITIES

By eating a diet of natural foods containing no toxins, drugs, or chemicals, and by routinely fasting in moderation, we can cleanse our colons so our bodies can "breathe" again. Humans consist of the same elements found in the earth. Fruits, nuts, grains, and vegetables contain the same elements.

When our diets consist mainly of foods laden with toxins, our bodies will begin to break down over time. However, when these foods are eaten in their natural state and not robbed of their life-giving properties through excessive processing or chemical additives, we can understand that "fruit is the meat, and the leaves are the medicine."

Here's a fun exercise to do from Dr. Christopher: Before you eat your next meal, take the food off your plate and plant it in the ground. In one row, plant the white bread, pot roast, and chocolate chip cookie. Don't forget the candy bar, potato chips, and soda Now in another row plant the potato, alfalfa, apples, grapes, and nuts, and see how they begin to sprout. The latter are living foods in their natural state. You will receive the secret of life from living foods in their wholesome and natural state. It is educational and useful to read labels for every food item you buy.

Most processed foods contain preservatives or additives like MSG which increase the shelf life or enhance the taste but are toxic to the body. Processed foods tend to have high levels of salt (sodium), refined sugar, and chemicals, all of which impede immune health and contribute to a variety of diseases. And it is widely known that most fruits and vegetables contain pesticides that were used by farmers to maximize the yield. Cut as much processed and pesticide-tainted food from your diet as possible.

Milk producers tell us how much milk we need in our daily lives. But milk creates mucus in our system which breeds infections and germs. Farmers give cows hormones, chemicals, and antibiotics to fatten them up and prevent them from getting sick. Those toxins are passed along to us through the meat and milk we take in. If you simply eliminate cow's milk and foods made from it, substituting other natural sources of Vitamin D and calcium in your diet, you may begin to see an improvement in your health.

DISCOVER YOUR INFINITE POSSIBILITIES

Processed foods like potato chips, bread, and pasta – in addition to containing toxic preservatives and additives for texture and taste – lose much of their nutritional value in processing. Even some foods marketed as health foods such as whole wheat bread lose much of their nutrition in processing. There are many books on the topic of "nutritionally dense" foods versus "energy-dense" or empty calorie foods like French fries, potato chips, and white bread if you wish to study further. The best diet includes mostly if not exclusively nutritionally dense whole foods that are not highly processed and have no additives.

Similarly, meat from animals that are naturally fed and not injected with hormones and antibiotics to increase the muscle mass or prevent illnesses is good for us in moderation. But meat from animals injected with those substances or fed genetically modified grains treated with pesticides will be toxic for us. Russia a few years ago refused our beef because it contained too much formaldehyde. Formaldehyde is a respiratory irritant that causes chest pain, shortness of breath and cancer according to American Cancer Society. The same year China refused our eggs because of the high arsenic content, and they are consumed by us.

Did you see labels on products; 'This product has been know to cause cancer in California.' Why are they selling it to consumers in other states?

Poor immune health, directly related to the foods we eat, has been linked to cancer, Type 2 Diabetes, and a variety of other physical problems.

The FDA is a contradiction. They permit drugs in our food and Water so others can make money off of us, unjust enrichment. They will be held accountable for the early deaths and unnecessary pain they caused others.

We must band together as citizens and stop the insanity.

DISCOVER YOUR INFINITE POSSIBILITIES
THE LAW OF FASTING

God instituted the Law of Fasting. It calls attention to the sin of gluttony by placing the body in subjection to the spirit. How humiliating it must be to a thoughtful person to be a slave to their appetites (or to any overwhelming and pernicious habit, desire, or passion for that matter)! Habitual fasting insures a spiritual strength and power we so greatly need. Fasting should always be accompanied by prayer, which will be discussed in a later section.

The will of God is for us to practice moderation in all things, including food. Fasting will bring us nearer to God and deepen our minds. It is this renewing of the mind and spirit that keeps us untainted by the sins of this world. The Law of the Fast combines belief, practice, and faith.

A one- or two-day natural juice fast is good for the body. Fresh organic fruit and vegetable juices will fill us up and give us life-sustaining minerals while helping our bodies purge toxins. Drinking plenty of spring distilled water – especially for those who are overweight – will flush salts from the system, thereby reducing blood pressure naturally. We can aid this process by eliminating all excess salt in our diets.

Greed is rampant in the food and pharmaceutical industries. Someone is getting rich off our diseased bodies. You say that you don't see Satan in your daily life? He has infiltrated your system, preventing you from thriving, thwarting the blessing you should be receiving. Refined sugar and chemicals from the food we eat are robbing our bodies of calcium and other life-giving minerals, aiding the degeneration process and impeding immune health.

We need to exercise our bodies.

Perhaps we do this by walking, jogging, swimming, dancing, or playing a sport such as a tennis. Remember to breathe deeply when exercising, as oxygen purifies the blood since it can be given the air impurities of modern times.

DISCOVER YOUR INFINITE POSSIBILITIES

The skin is the largest elimination organ of the body, and we should brush the skin daily to remove dead layers so it may breathe properly.

Be mindful of your feet. Did you know that the soles of your feet absorb what they come into contact with? If you want to test this, put some cayenne pepper on the soles of your feet.

You may find that it keeps you warm and keeps you awake! Even dyes from socks can enter the bloodstream. If the bloodstream is clean, no matter how many germs get into our bodies, our immune systems will be strong enough to protect us.

We need a proper diet, fresh air, sunshine, exercise, pure water, and proper rest to attune our bodies with nature, allowing the spirit to flow within us and leave impressions on our hearts and minds.

God has provided a remedy for every disease that might afflict us. Satan cannot afflict anyone with any disease for which God has not provided a remedy. If medical colleges would put forth the true remedies God has provided for us, they would cure all the ills of man!

It is easy to see Satan operating in our society through the greed in the food and pharmaceutical industries, keeping us overmedicated and full of disease-causing toxins. Consider consulting an herbalist or naturopathic physician to find out which herbal remedies can be substituted for their pharmaceutical counterparts.

Having clearly defined goals will give us the energy to purify our physical and emotional bodies and help us remain positive and focused.

With the Spirit as our guide, we can receive fine-tuning of our mind. A measure of happiness will be restored through a newly found method of living and thinking.

DISCOVER YOUR INFINITE POSSIBILITIES
POWER OF PRAYER

When we have prayer and the constant companionship of Spirit, we gain the ability to retain the light of a clear mind.

Today we must stop worshipping food, money, and material things and start worshipping God. It is not an easy task. Evil forces abound around us, and their chemicals are inside us. We must call upon God for strength.

We would do well to pray morning and evening, recognizing Him (or Her) in everything we do. We should ask for a blessing on the food we eat. We should change our habits first; then God will bless us with greater strength. Ask God for guidance. If our bodies and minds are in tune, He will answer us. Once we are spiritually in tune, if we have a decision to make, we can bring our decision to God. If it is the correct decision, we will feel it in our hearts. If we forget what we are praying for while we are in prayer, then we have received a sign that we made the wrong decision. We should change to the other decision and again take it to God. If it is the correct decision, we will think about it all the time and receive a warm feeling in our hearts. God confirmed it's the right decision.

As you do your one-day fast, go to a quiet place and kneel. If you do not feel the spirit of prayer, do not get up off your knees until you do.

Ask the Spirit for help. You may also ask in the name of our elder brother, Jesus Christ, for the enlightenment of mind and strength of spirit. As you return home, share your experience with others who are close to you.

Do we know how to listen to the small voice? It is said that if we want to communicate with God, we should pray. If we want God to communicate with us, we are to read the Scriptures of any house of worship (provided that they are translated correctly) and *be still*! The Scriptures give us the strength in our daily lives to overcome evil forces and our erroneous habits. We must quiet our minds to hear the still small voice in our hearts. *That is the spirit of God.*

DISCOVER YOUR INFINITE POSSIBILITIES

The prayerful person will set an example for all others. Do you know whether the prayer you have offered has ascended beyond the ceiling of the room? Prayer must be offered from the heart, try to avoid rote prayers.

We need to exercise prayer like we exercise our bodies. We must do so regularly to achieve maximum results. With the power of heaven to assist us, we can be successful in this mortal life in spite of our weaknesses. If we learn to ask in prayer, our financial, educational, economic, and physical conditions or limitations become insignificant.

DISCOVER YOUR INFINITE POSSIBILITIES
TRY IT GOD'S WAY FOR THIRTY DAYS.

Try this for thirty days: Orient yourself toward God and away from worldly concerns. Seek the help and guidance of God continuously through prayer and thought. Ask for forgiveness for the things you have done wrong. Look inside yourself and take inventory of your wrong doings. Ask for God's help in releasing resentments toward those who have wronged you.

If you find it difficult to believe in a Higher Power, you can preface your prayers with, "God, if you exist." At the same time, take in one week of high-quality mineral water in order to clean the billions of brain cells from aluminum.

After that, drink nothing but spring water. Do a natural juice fast one day a week or more if you can tolerate it. Volunteer in your community helping others who are less fortunate. Do these things and see if your mind becomes open to new way of thinking.

See if you become more creative in your thinking. You may notice habitual self-limiting thoughts arise in your consciousness. Be aware that those thoughts no longer serve you. Focus on inventing your future independent of what others have wanted for you. The groundwork you are setting through prayer and fasting, moderate exercise and proper diet will prepare you to receive the messages from your Higher Power.

DISCOVER YOUR INFINITE POSSIBILITIES
BECOME A BEACON TO OTHERS

Law of Expectations: The Pygmalion Effect

The correct way to motivate others, who in turn can motivate us, is Through the Pygmalion Effect, or through having higher expectations Of them that they have of themselves.

Pygmalion, according to Greek Mythology, sculpted a beautiful female statue and fell instantly and passionately in love with it. Infatuated with his statue, he would carry it from room to room with him and shower adoration upon it as though it were an actual living breathing woman. According to the myth, Aphrodite, the Goddess of Love, paid a visit to Pygmalion and breathed life into his statue, making it come alive.

In the play, 'Pygmalion" by George Bernard Shaw, (later renamed "My Fair Lady"),Professor Higgins knew he could talk to the very next person he met and motivate that person to do whatever he wanted. He believed he could befriend anyone at all – even the lowliest street woman in England – Eliza Doolittle – and teach her enough of the King's English and mannerisms to pass her off as a socialite at the King's Ball. His high expectations did have a similar outcome to the Pygmalion myth in that she became who he envisioned her to be. By expecting more of her than she did of herself, he demonstrated the Pygmalion Effect.

If you expect the best from people, more often than not, you will receive it. Expect the best from yourself and you will receive that too.

DISCOVER YOUR INFINITE POSSIBILITIES
Rosenthal Study

Dr. Rosenthal was a research scientist at UCLA. He went to a second grade classroom in a grammar school and asked the teacher to leave the classroom while he passed out and collected a test. He never actually graded the test, but he misled the teacher into believing he did. Then he identified two random students from the class and told the teacher that because they had scored the highest on the test, they were the brightest students in the classroom. Three months later Dr. Rosenthal went back to the classroom and discovered that the two random students he had identified had received A+ grades. He then repeated this experiment in an automotive machine shop at a junior high with the same results.

His notes reflected that during breaks, other students would go over to the supposedly smart students and ask them questions that they could not answer. In response, the two "smart" students studied harder because they now had a new expectation factor - or a Pygmalion Effect – to live up to.

In a second study, Dr. Rosenthal met with five professors at UCLA. He told them, "Professors, we don't want to get sued as a university, so we need to keep this confidential. You, five professors, have the highest IQ scores on campus. As an experiment, I am going to assign you the top fifty brightest students on campus. Just by your association with them, I know they will be challenged and will excel even more." Three months later Dr. Rosenthal checked back. The fifty students assigned to the five professors had the highest grades on campus. Dr. Rosenthal took the professors aside again and revealed the truth to them: "Professors, I want you to know that we picked these students randomly, but because you thought they were smart, you treated them like they were smart, and guess what? They lived up to the expectation factor you set for them!" One professor responded, "The students excelled because of our high IQs " To this, Dr. Rosenthal replied, "No, because we picked you five out at random, as well."

Take a moment and examine your expectations of your mate, your children, or your employer. What are your expectations for them?

DISCOVER YOUR INFINITE POSSIBILITIES

If you expect to go home to a grumpy mate and uncaring children, guess what you are going to find? How do you expect to find your employer when you go to work? Like Pygmalion, you are going to find whatever you expect.

Jesus Christ and all the Prophets expected more of us than we expect of ourselves.

The greatest power we have as human beings is the power to influence others for the good. You might prevent suicide merely with a smile or word of encouragement. What have you done today to brighten someone's life? Did you plant any seeds that a person might harvest later? Did you have a positive God-centered attitude?

The test of our soul's greatness is in our ability to comfort and console, to help others rather than solely helping ourselves.

What did you do today in God's kingdom?

Did you share your love of God with others?

Did you plant any seeds today that may be harvested later?

Do you have control over your emotions and physical health?

Are you ready to fast and pray for strength?

Are you ready to ask God to enlighten your mind as you read this.

Pray you will understand what is expected of you in this life.

DISCOVER YOUR INFINITE POSSIBILITIES
HOW WE CAME TO BE

We need to cry as Moses did, "Depart from me, Satan, for this one God I will worship is the God of glory!" Moses is the pride and pleasure of God and the object of His infinite creation. We are the literal offspring of God.

As such, we were created spiritually before we were created temporally – in time and space. God intended for Adam to fall as the only way several billion spirits could come to this planet. However, our spirit tabernacles (spirits before acquiring bodies) delayed their progress until we were given temporal bodies. Some of us were in the same classroom before we came here. That is why some people we've never met seem familiar to us.

We were required to subject ourselves to a lower plane of existence where we could acquire physical bodies. Now we must learn the spiritual laws for operating these bodies. Without physical bodies, we could not know joy.

Joy is an emotional marriage of the mind and body. In this life we are to learn to acquire to a limited degree the sweetness of joy. But a lasting fullness of joy can be obtained only when our bodies have been connected with our spirits forever. "Straight is the gate and narrow is the way, which leads unto life, and few that there be who find it."

Mortality is our conditioning against rebellious behavior. Understand that there are no shortcuts to exaltation. We must labor every day of our existence in the kingdom to build it up with a singleness of purpose to glorify Him.

We are here to choose between the bitterness of sin, procrastination, and rebellion and the sweetness of obedience. God said that as rapidly as we overcome evil, He would blot out the offense and would not hold it against us. This is the Principle of Repentance.

DISCOVER YOUR INFINITE POSSIBILITIES
PRINCIPLE OF REPENTANCE

We are all sinners.

As a teenager, I arranged an abortion for a girlfriend. I felt what I had done was wrong, but her father was very powerful, and she was embarrassed to tell him she was pregnant. I lived with the guilt for years, but God as a loving parent permitted me to atone by saving two lives: A girl drowning in a swimming pool and a young man who in a brief moment of insanity tried to kill his brother. He also permitted me to save my own life, as well as the lives of anyone who is touched by my writings. It is my firm belief that God is in control, and nothing happens without a purpose divined by Him.

How do we think we are going to progress in God's kingdom if we sin? We all define sin differently, and we have all sinned. Jesus Christ was born to bear the sins of the world. It is human to err, but now that we realize the -position we are in, how can we be better?

Our behaviors over time create our character, and our character defines us. Good character means living in integrity or being righteous in all actions, even when no one is watching. This includes telling the truth even when it is uncomfortable to do so. A lie is any attempt to deceive even by omission.

Most people claim they cannot be truthful at all times, that it is impossible. Deliberately lying and deceiving others causes Spirit to withdraw from us. The world is so evil that some people cannot even keep the basic Ten Commandments. They justify murder, adultery, thievery, dishonesty, slavery, and exploitation of others.

Central Florida Reception Center (CFRC) Prison Program

I have volunteered my time giving free seminars to the unemployed, underemployed, and prison inmates. One such program was the Central Florida Prison Transition Program, a non-denominational program I created to help inmates transition into the community. On the first day of class, I asked the inmates two questions: The first was, "What are you going to do when you get out?"

DISCOVER YOUR INFINITE POSSIBILITIES

Many answer that they will "get a big hit," meaning get high on drugs or alcohol. The second question I asked was, "Where are you goingto go when you get out?"

Usually, they respond that they will go back to the same unhealthy environment. "Back to my homies." After the 100-hour program, the answers are emphatically different: When asked, "What are you going to do when you get out?" a typical response would be, "Have you pick me up and help me find work or open a business, and live in one of your transitional homes." They come to realize they are a temple of God and that they must break Satan's hold on them. Prison guards reported that after going through the program, the inmates changed, and the guards felt safer around them. The inmates showed more respect. Incidents dropped to zero!

Are you trying to change but find it difficult? Let me give you a challenge I give to hardened criminals in prison. Try it God's way for thirty days! Commit to do this and see if God pours out a blessing upon you that makes you cry out, "You have changed my life by giving me so much."

DISCOVER YOUR INFINITE POSSIBILITIES
TO BE TRULY REPENTANT, YOU NEED TO MAINTAIN A REPENTANT ATTITUDE AT ALL TIMES.

You must be genuinely remorseful for the sin you committed, with a firm resolve never to sin again, even if it means you must leave your friends or the environment that led you to commit that sin in the first place. This is the Principle of Repentance. Jesus tells us in the Scriptures that when the earth is celestialized, "Repentance shall be hidden from mine eyes." In other words, this is the time. If you wait, it may be too late.

An exact quote from an inmate who was a C.P.A., and participated in my Florida Prison Transitional Program: "All I wanted to do was get out and earn money. Now, going through this transition program, I want to serve the Lord."

Since the nature of an empty mind is to fill itself, new creative thoughts and goals will quickly replace the discarded, undesirable patterns. To fail at this point is to slip backward. The human mind will keep busy with something. If we fail to steer the mind in the proper direction, it will continue to operate, but it will wander out of control, returning to the same habitual ruts.

The Wagon Master didn't have to pay attention to where he was going. All he had to do was put his wagon's wheels in the ruts where everyone else went before, he just followed the ruts. The secret to life is to ride the ridges of life and be aware of other opportunities you may have never thought of. An intelligent person will look at all the options available, which most people don't' know because of their prior programming.

DISCOVER YOUR INFINITE POSSIBILITIES

We need the courage to change the things we can. We see people who are unable to take decisive action because they feel their difficulties are the result of circumstances. Such an attitude prevents them from becoming the people they are capable of being. We are not helpless to confront the problems of daily living. We can change the stage of life if we set the proper goals and make a commitment to achieve them. We will be able to control the circumstances, rather than allowing the circumstances to control us.

If we follow all of His Commandments, we will be blessed in having Him direct our lives. We have free will to understand and accept this universal law.

DISCOVER YOUR INFINITE POSSIBILITIES

.   **Most of us live in mental handcuffs, failing to realize we have the freedom to choose.**

My life today compared with the mess it was yesterday shows great progress. As the days come and go, I will continue to progress and grow in a greater understanding of the Scriptures. If I were merely to read the Scriptures daily and conduct private and family prayers, if I ask God to help me better fulfill my mission here on earth, I will be fulfilling His will and not mine. We are all going to die! Today is here with the promise of what we make of it. We know the past will be remembered only through pleasurable memories if the present is lived following what is expected of us by Spirit. The present holds the seeds of eternity.

If you are living within God's plan, the present moment offers an opportunity for a little touch of heaven. Those who still do not live by all of His laws must change their thinking. We forget that this moment is all we have. All we have in this life is a certain amount of time which diminishes every minute of every hour.

DISCOVER YOUR INFINITE POSSIBILITIES
Do not harbor any ill feelings in your heart towards any living creature.

You need not become the policemen or policewomen of the world. Instead, learn to take the beam out of your eye. We have the uncanny ability to create scotomas or blind spots to our wrongdoings. Nothing is quite as contemptible as idle gossip uttered with injurious intent. He who taketh up a reproach against his neighbor is in great danger of losing the spirit of God.

See that you do not judge wrongfully, for that "which ye judged shall be judged." We should not permit ourselves to go from day to day with a spirit of fault-finding in our hearts against anyone. Brotherly love has no room for bitterness; it must be removed. We should seek to love one another and to sustain one another as children of God and as brothers and sisters, regardless of race, color, religion, gender, sexual orientation, or age.

We too frequently see a disposition in our children to make fun of the unfortunate. This is entirely wrong! Such a spirit as this should never be encouraged in children.

How are we to love our neighbor as we love ourselves? It is the simplest of all tasks. Waiting for someone else to step in and help another is not the way of Spirit. We should treat everyone as if they are four years of age, with no hidden agenda other they just helping one another travel the road of progression. God is not pleased with those who fail to acknowledge His hand in everything connected to their success or those who take full credit themselves.

DO NOT DESTROY LIFE WANTONLY.

Humans should not kill animals unless we need them for sustenance.

DISCOVER YOUR INFINITE POSSIBILITIES
HOME AND FAMILY

Let love, peace, kindness, charity, and sacrifice for others abound in your families. Become a specialist in truth.

A home is not a home in the eye of God unless there dwell perfect confidence and love, one that follows the Gospel plan.

As the tree is judged by its fruit, so we also judge the home by our children. The main aim is not to heap up material wealth, which draws us further from the truth. The spiritual ideal is the creation of soul wealth, the consciousness of noble achievement, and an outflow of love and helpfulness.

I have made many mistakes in my home life. I thought I was a good father because I provided material things to my children, while spending time away from them. I, too, was caught in the trap of materialism.

Now, years later when the mansion is gone, the travel is not affordable, the excess and fancy cars and expensive possessions are gone, no one remembers dad who was traveling and working hard to support the lavish lifestyle. I am alone in the world because I could not continue to keep my family in the lifestyle to which they were accustomed. This was my responsibility. I thought I was doing well

DISCOVER YOUR INFINITE POSSIBILITIES

working hard for them, but I was never at home. What they needed was a father to spend time with them, not a money tree.

We must follow *all* of His Commandments.

The ancient people of Noah's day needed to be told not to kill and steal; they found nothing wrong with these acts. The same is true today; many people see nothing wrong in taking advantage of another. The spirit of God cannot reside within us unless we are doing what is right. A truly repentant sinner will eagerly seek to learn what is required of him or her. God has promised forgiveness unto those who truly repent. All who prepare themselves for repentance will be led by the humbling and softening influence of the Holy Spirit. However, repentance becomes more difficult as the skin becomes more willful. No one is justified in postponing their efforts to repent. To procrastinate the day of repentance is to place ourselves deliberately under the power of Satan.

You are the salt of the earth and in whom is vested the light of God. You must let your light shine, individually and collectively. Every person should not only experience this light within themselves but should shine it so brightly that others may see and understand it. The future of God's children and the world rests upon your shoulders. All the prophets who ever walked on the face of the earth taught, "First, learn how to love God. Have gratitude for the experiences you have had on this earth. Second, love yourself and your spiritual brothers and sisters." It is that simple. It has been made complicated because humankind has rewritten history and divided us by membership into religious sects. Membership equates to money and control. Man has programmed you for his benefit. These techniques have been used throughout history. Stalin, Lenin, Hitler, and Mussolini have all used them to control the masses, it has been happening in the U.S. today.

Nazism believed Hitler was the savior, the Third Reich the son, and the Nazi Party, the holy ghost. The same subconscious subliminal techniques Hitler, Stalin, Lenin and Mussolini used are being used on the United States Citizens since 1945 by using subliminal techniques your conscious mind isn't aware that your subconscious

DISCOVER YOUR INFINITE POSSIBILITIES

mind is receiving. I teach the same techniques in my sales and customer service classes.

It's how to get into someone's reticular formation, it's located at the base of the brain stem. It's a filtering system for your mind. It let's in anything of value or a threat, anything else, we build scotomas, blind spots.

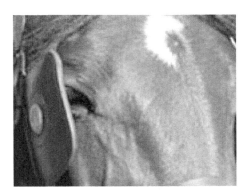

We don't pay attention to it. We are creatures of conditioned reflex, just like Pavlov's Dog. We react because of the habits we have retained from childhood. We are taught this is the only way based on traditions. If dad's a mechanic, that's what the son will probably become.

We need to step out of our comfort zone to see all the possibilities.

If you have sleepless night thinking about what you read, I would have fulfilled the mission to make people aware that change is the hardest thing to do in the world because we don't want to think about it. There is an easier way to make money by using your brains instead of your back. Let's explore the possibilities which you have, but are unaware of.

Let me help you start your own business, if you don't know what kind, I'll give you a list of businesses you can start with no money or personal liability. Let me help to bring you to a higher level of intelligence and a more rewarding life for your family.

DISCOVER YOUR INFINITE POSSIBILITIES

Your reward may be a trip to the mountains, or an around the world cruise, something you actually worked for and are enjoying the rewards of the fruit of your creative forces.

Dr. Eisenstein had said: "Creativity and Imagination are more important than education, because I can show you things you cannot see."

DISCOVER YOUR INFINITE POSSIBILITIES
GODLY GOALS VERSUS MATERIAL GOALS

Do you worry about your family? When you attain a higher perception of who you are and what you are to accomplish on earth, you will soon be worried not just about your immediate family, but also about your city, nation, and all of our brothers and sisters in the world.

We must all be thinkers and workers, men and women who weigh matters in our minds; we must study and understand the spiritual principles so we may conduct ourselves with the spirit of loyalty and devotion, together with love for the work of building up the kingdom of God.

Everyone should be laboring in God's vineyard for their good and as far as possible for the good of others. Each individual must be diligent in performing their duty, and in keeping themselves pure and untainted from the world in a non-judgmental way.

If you are thinking in a higher plane, you would do good to worry about Mother Earth and what we have done to her. Soon she will not be able to sustain life because of human greed

God has brought me to Pueblo, Colorado to transform this city from one with a lack of vision to one that will be a beacon of light for the rest of the world. My vision for Pueblo Colorado is that we collectively will be the catalyst for changing a city's culture and will bring the citizens of Pueblo together in unity from all religions and walks of life so everyone will benefit financially and spiritually to a new way of thinking as old as time.

The young person who would cope with the world would be full of vigor and fresh for the bottle of life. He will find his strength in living according to the word of God, for the promise is that all "who remember to keep and do these sayings, waking in obedience to the Commandments, shall receive health in their navel and marrow in their bones and shall find wisdom and great treasures of knowledge, even hidden treasures, and shall run and not be weary, and shall walk and not faint, and I The Lord, give unto them a promise,

DISCOVER YOUR INFINITE POSSIBILITIES
that the Destroying Angel shall pass by them, as the children of Israel, and not slay them."

"Failure" is a word that should be unknown. Do not say it cannot be done; we must be determined to do our duty. Remember, God raised prophets to lay the foundations of this work and did His work through them. God, if we are in tune, will direct us so that we may fulfill our mission here on earth. With fulfillment of our mission, we will return to His presence.

We are called to preach to the world and to declare the truth. If someone disagrees with us, that is okay; we did our part by planting the seed. Love them anyway.

We get closer to God when we start loving strangers as much as we love our own family; then we realize that we are all family.

DISCOVER YOUR INFINITE POSSIBILITIES
GODLY GOALS VERSUS MATERIAL GOALS

Do you worry about your family? When you attain a higher perception of who you are and what you are to accomplish on earth, you will soon be worried not just about your immediate family, but also about your city, nation, and all of our brothers and sisters in the world.

We must all be thinkers and workers, men and women who weigh matters in our minds; we must study and understand the spiritual principles so we may conduct ourselves with the spirit of loyalty and devotion, together with love for the work of building up the kingdom of God.

Everyone should be laboring in God's vineyard for their good and as far as possible for the good of others. Each individual must be diligent in performing their duty, and in keeping themselves pure and untainted from the world in a non-judgmental way.

If you are thinking in a higher plane, you would do good to worry about Mother Earth and what we have done to her. Soon she will not be able to sustain life because of human greed

God has brought me to Pueblo, Colorado to transform this city from one with a lack of vision to one that will be a beacon of light for the rest of the world. My vision for Pueblo Colorado is that we collectively will be the catalyst for changing a city's culture and will bring the citizens of Pueblo together in unity from all religions and walks of life so everyone will benefit financially and spiritually to a new way of thinking as old as time.

The young person who would cope with the world would be full of vigor and fresh for the bottle of life. He will find his strength in living according to the word of God, for the promise is that all "who remember to keep and do these sayings, waking in obedience to the Commandments, shall receive health in their navel and marrow in their bones and shall find wisdom and great treasures of knowledge, even hidden treasures, and shall run and not be weary, and shall walk and not faint, and I The Lord, give unto them a promise,

DISCOVER YOUR INFINITE POSSIBILITIES

that the Destroying Angel shall pass by them, as the children of Israel, and not slay them."

"Failure" is a word that should be unknown. Do not say it cannot be done; we must be determined to do our duty. Remember, God raised prophets to lay the foundations of this work and did His work through them. God, if we are in tune, will direct us so that we may fulfill our mission here on earth. With fulfillment of our mission, we will return to His presence.

We are called to preach to the world and to declare the truth. If someone disagrees with us, that is okay; we did our part by planting the seed. Love them anyway.

We get closer to God when we start loving strangers as much as we love our own family; then we realize that we are all family.

DISCOVER YOUR INFINITE POSSIBILITIES
THE AFTERLIFE

What we become after we leave our bodies will result directly from the lives we lead now. After death, we will either enjoy or loathe the fruits of our doing. Those who strive earnestly will enjoy being reunited with their eternal families.

In the early church, before man rewrote the Scriptures, Pythagoras, the father of mathematics taught reincarnation. However, man has changed the original teachings to dispel the notion of reincarnation. According to the original teachings, we return again and again until as humans we have evolved to the highest plane. A human being has evolved to the highest plane. An embryo is the stage of human development that is closest to God because it has not yet been subjected to the conditioning of the earthly life.

Dr. Brian Wise University of Miami has published numerous books on his research. How does a seven years old girl remembers past lives in different countries and speaks various languages under regression. Or the Sleeping Prophet, Edwin Casey, with thousands of testimonials.

There must be hundreds if not thousands like me who have had at least one out of body experience. We know beyond a doubt the spirit goes on after we drop this outer shell.

Do you know where you were before you were permitted to arrive in earthly form? You dwelt in God's kingdom. Your spirit was in His presence surrounded by your brother and sister spirits. Don't you remember? The veil of forgetfulness is thin for some of us.

As the time arrived for you to come to earth, you heard a voice say, "Go son and daughter to yonder lower world and take upon thee a tabernacle, and work out thy probation." "But remember, you go on this condition: You are to forget all the things you ever saw or knew in this spirit world. You are not going to know or remember anything. You must go and become one of the most helpless of all beings that I have created, while in your infancy subjected to sickness, pain, tears, mourning, sorrow, and death.

DISCOVER YOUR INFINITE POSSIBILITIES

But when truth shall touch the chords of
your heart, they will vibrate; then intelligence shall illuminate your mind and shed its luster in your soul, and you shall begin to understand the things you once knew; you shall then begin to understand and know the object of your creation. Go, and be faithful as thou has been in their first estate."

All men and women must know their mortality, and so it is important to understand where we are going. It is reasonable to suppose that God would reveal something about death. It is a subject we should study more than any other. We ought to study it by day and night, for the world is ignorant of its true condition.

Life is very short. Therefore, everything we do we must keep in the perspective of eternity. Life does continue beyond death. I have been there and God wanted me to return to fulfill the measure of my existence. Death is part of God's plan. It enables us to examine our own life experiences in our progression so that we may attain eternal immortal life. For this reason, it is crucial to living by the spirit here on earth and obey God's will so that we may live for all eternity with our families.

We have an unseen cheering crowd composed of past and future generations rooting for us to behave righteously because their future happiness depends on the decisions we make in this
earthly life. Some of us recognize them as guardian angels. If we honor our mission here, they will help us achieve it. But we must follow all of God's Commandments – not the Commandments set by humankind who build churches to receive unjust enrichment.

DISCOVER YOUR INFINITE POSSIBILITIES
WE ARE NOT MORTALS HAVING A SPIRITUAL EXPERIENCE, BUT RATHER,
WE ARE SPIRITS HAVING A MORTAL EXPERIENCE.

We must learn to overcome temptations of the flesh, our temper, our tongue, and our disposition to indulge in all things God has forbidden if we want to progress into the celestial kingdom of God. This lifetime is the time in which we are to repent. Do not let any of us imagine we die without having overcome these corruptions, thinking we can slough off our sins and evil tendencies in the grave.

A good illustration of this is a scene from the movie, Ghost. Patrick Swayze's character was in the subway talking to the ghost of a man who had died. The dead man was trying to obtain cigarettes, just as he had done in his mortal life!

Habits remain with us after this life, which is why it is so important to overcome them. It is much easier to change during our mortal life than after our spirits leave our bodies. Once the spirit leaves the body and is judged, it may be sent into outer darkness where it (we) will remain as long as it is needed for us to understand the mistakes we have made and how our decisions on earth have affected others.

Any man or woman can do more to conform to the laws of God in one year on earth than they can in a thousand years in outer darkness.

This life is the time to repent! Every person who is putting off until the next life the task of correcting and overcoming the weaknesses of the flesh are sentencing themselves to years of bondage, that is, if God even allows that person another chance, for this might be their final call. No man or woman will come forth in the Resurrection until they have completed their work. Those who comply in this life are shortening their sentences, for every one of us will have a matter of years in the spirit state to attain salvation.

If we are following God's plan on earth, then when we die, we are immediately conscious that we have changed our condition, and most of us who die are met beyond the veil by a welcoming committee, which often consists of our guardian angel and/or

DISCOVER YOUR INFINITE POSSIBILITIES

deceased relatives. We retain the same senses and sensations we knew as mortal beings. We dwell in family groups and remain aware of relationships from generation to generation.

The spirit being retained human form with head, arms, hands, torso, legs, etc.

Though we are given free will, if we are to attain salvation, we must turn that will over to God. We must understand that the will of God can be manifested on earth as it is in heaven only when we resign completely so that His will may be manifested through us. We must not be selfish; we must not assert our will against the will of God.

If we are to return to peace and innocence, we must follow His plan, remembering always that we have the free agency to decide which path we choose.

God has promised that if we come unto Him in humility, our weaknesses will become strengths. When we pray, we pull down the powers of heaven; the talents and abilities we already possess of which we may be unaware will come forward and be greatly magnified. Our ultimate achievements in this life will be determined more by our ability to pray and communicate fervently with God than by our reliance solely on natural abilities.

DISCOVER YOUR INFINITE POSSIBILITIES

I pray that we do not fall into a rut and become stagnant in our mortal progression, living day to day, never growing or changing in our relation with our Higher Power. If we are slothful servants, the lives of others are unaffected by our presence and conduct. We will exist only to satisfy our daily needs. This attitude does not come from God but man influenced by wicked spirits. The Scriptures refer to wicked spirits as "foul spirits, spirits who affect persons in the flesh and engender various diseases in the human system." Some of these spirits are adulterous and suggest to the mind all manner of lasciviousness, all kinds of evil thought and temptation.

If men and women fail to become sanctified and purified in this life, they will proceed into a world where they will face greater contest with the Devil than they ever had with him here on earth. Some of us are privileged to know beforehand when we are to pass beyond the veil.

Most recent to my knowledge is the passing of Ofa Fauna. Three weeks before his sudden death at 42 years of age, he warned a church group to be prepared: "The work is great on the other side of the veil. God can call you at any time; we must be worthy and stand ready to serve Him." Ofa left a legacy of honesty and dedication to building up God's kingdom rather than his own. He dedicated his life to God by voluntarily building houses at no charge for the homeless. He was and still is known as a man of action and courage! I pray that when I complete my earthly mission, I am worthy enough to see Ofa, as friendships like his are eternal.

When we die, we step out of this sphere and into another. Perhaps, Instead of calling it "death," we should call it "another birth," or as some cultures refer to it, "dropping of the body."

DISCOVER YOUR INFINITE POSSIBILITIES

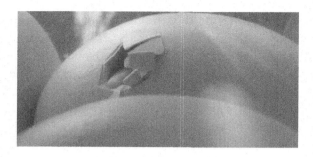

It's like a baby chick pecking out of his shell.

Spending eternity with those you love will be a joyful reunion. Christ said to the sinner, "Today you will be with me in Paradise." We must follow all of God's Commandments to be united with our families for all eternity. We will live with the consequences of our actions and decisions. It may be our hell we create by our actions in this life.

We need to carry with us the spirit of prayer to help us perform our duties in life. We must understand that we are utterly dependent upon our God; we are helpless without Him. How little can we do without His merciful providence on our behalf?

A single spear of grass cannot grow without the help of God. We have to use His earth. We must avail ourselves of the benefits of His soil, His air and sunshine, and the moisture that He provides for us to produce even a single blade of grass. The same applies to everything that ministers to our existence in the world. Why should we not love Him with all our heart, mind ,and strength, since he has given us life? Since he has formed us in His likeness? Since He has placed us here that we may become like His only begotten son? Since he wishes for us that we may inherit the glory, exaltation, and rewards provided for every one of His children? The very power of understanding is one of the many gifts bestowed upon us by God and is what separates us from animals. Life, intelligence, wisdom, judgment, and power to reason are some of the other gifts God has provided.

DISCOVER YOUR INFINITE POSSIBILITIES
BAPTISM

Baptism into a house of worship is the gateway leading into the fold of Christ. It is an act of obedience. In the early church, this was done through immersion in water. This signifies the covenant entered into between the repentant sinner and God which the person will observe all his or her life. Baptism symbolizes being cleansed in a watery grave. For the one being baptized, the sins will not rise with them, and they will enter into a new life with God.

When my eight-year-old son was baptized, he asked, coming out of the water, "Who were all those people in white?" I explained that those were his cheering crowd. "It was like a crowd at a football game, but those people were our relatives who have passed away or are yet to be born. They are all cheering for us to do the right thing. Their future depends on the decisions you will make every day. Those decisions will affect not only you but also those yet to be born." "Just as your Dad on earth loves you, please realize your Father in heaven loves you thousands of times more than your earthly Dad, and that if you follow all the Commandments you will return to the joys of eternity with all our family."

God has sent many prophets throughout the ages in different parts of the world. They all brought the same message: Love God first and love your neighbor as yourself.

A prophet is merely a witness, not a reformer. He or she is sent to teach the world rather than to criticize it. Paul, one of the apostles, was a great example. What did Christ and the apostles say that drove men to stone the apostles and crucify Christ in a fit of rage? They simply reported what they had seen and heard; that was all. As soon as the apostles said, "We are witnesses of these things," the high priests were angered because the truth they spoke threatened the priests' position. They took counsel to slay them. "We know Abraham is our father, and Moses is one of the prophets."
Christ himself had been charged as a false prophet, a wandering wise man, a so-called lunatic fanatic. Everyone must know for himself that Jesus is the Christ. No one is expected to believe that the Gospel is true because some official says so.

DISCOVER YOUR INFINITE POSSIBILITIES
Every person must experience these truths for themselves. The spirit of revelation and discernment must be in every individual.

The men who persecuted Christ could cite Scripture to justify all their actions and words. The Scripture was their only authority. They failed to realize that what Christ spoke was Scripture.
People argue endlessly about religion. But arguing solves nothing because religion has nothing to do with the truth.

DISCOVER YOUR INFINITE POSSIBILITIES
INDEPENDENCE VERSUS ENTITLEMENT

Every man and woman ought to possess the spirit of independence, a self-sustaining spirit that would prompt him or her to say when they are in need, "I am willing to give my labor in exchange for that which you give me."

It is wrong in the eyes of God for a person to think the world owes them a living. There is no great need in this world for physically and mentally able men and women not to work.

The Power of Directing Our Thoughts

Attitudes and desires are the direct results of our thoughts. When we choose to direct our thoughts unwisely, we leave the dimensions of the mind that control our desires open to suggestions. A mind unfocused will fill itself with anything that comes across its path; most of our thoughts have no lasting value and will draw us further away from God. We open our minds to the control of evil temptations. We have the free agency to direct our thoughts toward an eternal perspective or risk having them hijacked by evil thoughts. This is why many people believe that circumstances control their lives. If people want to change their thinking, all they have to do is set a Godly goal and commit to keeping it.

The spirit of God will be present and will bear witness to our humility if we put forth the effort. The spirit of God will flee if there is contention, for the spirit of contention does not come from God.

DISCOVER YOUR INFINITE POSSIBILITIES
Our Total Existence Should Be Goal-Oriented.

We must have goals to make progress. As in any athletic pursuit, working toward a goal set the mind in a higher plane and forces us to do our best. Goals should always make us reach, stretch, and strain. They should force us out of our comfort zone.

A goal in order for it to be a goal needs to be specific, quantifiable and most urgently, a completion date, or it will never get done.

In our relationship with God, we must be specific in our prayers and pray regularly. We will find that our prayers will become more earnest and will be sustained by faith. We will begin to feel the power of faith in our lives when we have been successful in maintaining the necessary mental discipline coupled with righteous living for several consecutive weeks. We will never experience the power of heaven unless we are willing to maintain our efforts over some time.

We must decide to paddle the canoe upstream; we must take the oar right now and start rowing if we want to take charge of our lives and positively influence the lives of those around us. You need to be on higher ground to pull someone up.

Don't procrastinate! Put this book down. Go to a quiet place and kneel if you can. Pray to the Supreme God of all the Universes to enlighten your mind so that you may understand. If you don't know how to pray, just keep kneeling and remain kneeling until you feel the spirit of prayer in your heart.

We all want to join the eternal family consisting of our ancestors, grandparents, parents, children, and generations still to be born. Each one of us alone is responsible for our eternal salvation. Each of us will stand alone at the Judgment Bar. Jesus Christ will be there – not to condemn, but to advocate for us. Suppose we were standing at the Judgment Bar right now.

We would see a movie of our lives – the good and the bad – including those actions we may not have considered as good or bad

DISCOVER YOUR INFINITE POSSIBILITIES

at the time. We may not realize how our previous earthly decisions affected others' lives. This is what will be shown. What about the person we bullied? Did they harm themselves because of our harsh words? What about the person we argue with? The one we mistreated? When they arrived at home, did they take their frustration out on their mate or children? What would we be thinking at that point? "I wish I could go back and live my life over! I wouldn't make the same mistakes again."

"PLEASE LET ME GO BACK AND BE A POSITIVE INFLUENCE IN PEOPLE'S LIVES."

God loves us so much that He permits some of us a second, third, or even a millionth chance.

Is it possible that we are here again to make up for past transgressions? Every person is born a spirit child of God. God doesn't want to lose any of us. Even though we live in God's world, some of us are led astray and adopt a rebellious attitude. We are here to learn gratitude.

It is terrible for men and women to neglect their duties so grossly that their misconduct will result in evil, for which some will be powerless to make restitution.

DISCOVER YOUR INFINITE POSSIBILITIES
HOW TO FIND YOUR MISSION IN LIFE
To progress, we must conform to all the requirements of God.

Men and women who turn over their lives to God will find out that He can make a lot more out of their lives than they can on their own. He will deepen their joys, expand their vision, quicken their minds, strengthen their muscles, lift their spirits, multiply their blessings, and increase their opportunities. He will also comfort their souls, raise friends, and pour out peace. Whoever will lose his life to God by serving others will find the windows of heaven pouring out blessings that will make that person cry out, "You have given me so much; I feel I am unable to receive."

It is through our efforts that we will have a clear understanding of how faith governs the powers of heaven. Many people say they would like to play the piano. Yet in reality, they would never pay the price of practicing every day for years to perfect the talent. One must have diligence and commitment to make a change.
I am 74 years old, with a limited life expectancy.

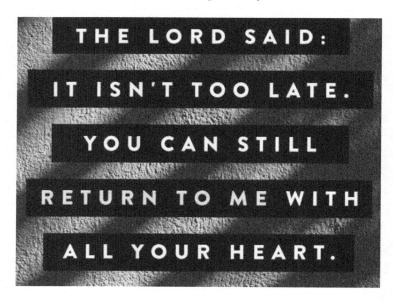

I didn't start receiving God's message until I was 58.

What is our mission in life? Have we been sidetracked again?

DISCOVER YOUR INFINITE POSSIBILITIES

Are we ready to recommit to God that we will review our lives Objectively with an open mind?

Our egos may prevent us from doing so. The person who thinks they have arrived has only just begun their journey. There is nothing which a person can possess in this world that will bring more comfort, hope and faith than an acknowledgment of the existence of God, the courage to defend it, and the opportunity to serve humankind.

Most of us confuse activity with accomplishment. Processionary caterpillars are so busy following each other that they might miss out on food and water, though it may be nearby. They will starve to death for failing to be focused on the life-sustaining things.

"Owe no man anything except to love each other, for he who loves the other man has fulfilled the law."

Find a person who performs their duties honestly in society, and I will show you a person full of the spirit of God. The full appreciation of the Gospel can only be achieved by those who face their weaknesses and limitations. We need to begin with a willingness to discover and honestly recognize the areas in our own lives where we can grow. When our fears prevent us from being charitable, we must not excuse ourselves with the common remark, "I have to take care of myself, don't I?" An excuse of this type is merely a protective wall behind which we hide our inner inadequacies.

A strong wind is no threat to a vigorous lone tree growing on a prairie – one whose root system has pushed deep into the soil during many a summer storm. But visit a grove of giant fir trees in the Oregon forest where giant trees have supported themselves for centuries, and isolate one tree apart from the others. Then wait until some winter night when a storm is raging.
This tree which has weathered dozens of such tempests in the company of its strong neighbor trees is now unprotected. Ill-prepared to withstand the high winds, this tree will crash thunderously to the ground! This illustrates that no person is an island.

DISCOVER YOUR INFINITE POSSIBILITIES

Do not call a person a weakling because they fail. If they had known beforehand that they possessed that weakness, they would have taken precautions to strengthen themselves for the storm ahead. One should be thankful for the person who stumbles, for, in their stumbling, those of us who follow are warned of the loose flagstone in life's staircase which we all must climb.

True love is not a matter of romance; it is a matter of anxious concern for others. Christ lived his life by this principle. He is our elder brother who suffered and died for us so we may live. Sacrificing His life for us upon the Cross of Calvary, He left behind a message that is embedded in everyone's mind. Even if they don't believe in Christ, they know Him.

DISCOVER YOUR INFINITE POSSIBILITIES
OUR MISSION IN THIS EARTHLY LIFE IS TO BRING HUMANITY TO A HIGHER SPIRITUAL LEVEL.

We are moving from Homo Sapiens to Homo Luminous, or human Beings seeing the physical world at a much higher spiritual level. We can reverse the trend of materialism that encourages people to take advantage of each other. Mastery of our insights lets us access the higher spiritual plane we are all trying to achieve.

We need to realize we are part of God's plan – to know good from evil and light from darkness – and to serve the greatest Supreme Being in all the universes, rather than be limited to this illusionary materialistic world in which we worship money, even if we have to lie, cheat, steal, and kill to get it.

Jesus left behind a religious movement radically different from both traditional Judaism and Roman Paganism. The new religion promised neither riches nor power, but prioritized loving God.

God is not pleased with a one world government to enrich a political military system in the name of religion. All political cults co-opt liturgical rubrics in order to legitimize themselves and fulfill a human desire to worship.

Jesus was asked which commandment is the greatest of all the Commandments. He replied, "Thou shall love the Lord thy God with all thy heart and with thy soul and thy mind. This is the first and greatest Commandment; the second like unto it, Thou shall love they neighbor as thyself."

Jesus relentlessly attacked hypocrisy and spiritual posing.

DISCOVER YOUR INFINITE POSSIBILITIES
YOUR INFINITE POSSIBILITIES

I have written this book to activate that part of you who remembers who you are and why you are here. I hope that these writings will catalyze to open your mind to all of the possibilities you have. What you do with this information is up to you. You and you alone carry the responsibility to make changes in your life. Life is a participant sport, not a spectator sport.

Accept personal accountability and you will recognize your infinite possibilities.

I have been inspired by God to write this book out of love and Concern that we all should have for one another.

I testify before God and humanity that the spirit of God used me to write this book.

I love you with all the love of the Lord.

Lou Principe

Made in the USA
Columbia, SC
01 June 2020